MW00976815

dear reader-

i began writing poetry at 13. originally, it was a coping mechanism after an attempted suicide in july of 2013 left me feeling unable to process all of the emotions inside of me. the idea for the *journey in words* project did not come about until the summer of 2017. since then, i have been doing my best to bring it to completion. and now we are here.

thank you for purchasing my book. this is my first book, and i won't lie to you, i am quite nervous about it being out in the world. it is a brutally honest glimpse into my life, and i am sending it out for anyone to view.

as i sit here and read these words, and watch my progression over the years one more time in my final week before publishing- writing this letter to you- i am filled with a sense of pride. reading this and watching the slow improvement, in both the quality of my poetry and of my life, makes me realize how far i have come.

when i was writing these poems, i wasn't able to see the little bits and pieces of progress i was making. but now that i have pulled this together, i can watch myself grow over the span of years.

it is important that you know that with anything you do in life, progress takes time. my poems were not perfect at 13. they are not perfect now. but they are far better. (as you will discover.) had i died that night in the summer of 2013, i never would have gotten to improve as much as i have.

but i didn't. and i didn't stop writing. i kept writing because it was something i felt in my soul, and something i needed to get better.

and now, here you are. reading my words. dear reader, i hope they help you. and i hope that you keep doing whatever you are doing.

far too often, we suffer alone. here is my gift to you.

i love you.

-k.

trigger warnings: rape, suicide, assault, abuse, depression, anxiety, self-harm.

this one is for the girl that i was, the girl that i am, and the girl i will be.

PART ONE- the fire

"i love you"
there are things in this world that scare me,
and there are things in this world that leave me sleepless,
breathless,
panicked,
paranoid.
heights scare me.
love falls in the second category.
because i fell in love
because he was wonderful
because he never wanted to hurt me
he never felt any malice towards me
because he was just as lost and confused as i was
he was just trying to figure things out
so he could protect me
but he didn't protect me
he hurt me

you must be careful
with the decisions you make
because you are left with them forever.
sometimes
a wrong decision
and you are left with the feeling
of an iv seeping into your veins
and the memory
of your mother crying
and the sound
of the sirens in the background
you are left holding that
every july
for the rest of your life.

how could you
forget about me?

when you took me
to the playground
under the stars
by the pool you
spent a summer working at
and we laid there
together
and you told me
sometimes you went there
to sit and think,
how can you
forget about me?

and so in love were we with the rain
that we threw ourselves into the sea, begging for more strength
begging for more water
begging for more love

and so in love were we with the stars
that we threw ourselves into the holes of the earth, begging for more knowledge
begging for more beauty
begging for more light

and so in love were we with the high
that we threw ourselves into the drinks
begging for less pain

and so in love were we with love
that we threw ourselves into the men and the sweat

begging to be worthy
begging to be loved
begging

each inch of my skin is a warzone and my head is the tattered remains of a battlefield between
my thoughts and the voices
fighting and kicking and shooting until all that is left is fire and the echo of tears i was once
capable of shedding
my eyes betray nothing; you do not see the wars i am losing every night
i claw at my own skin until the stinging takes away from the pounding in my head and i smile so
hard that everybody only sees the brightness
and not the blood i am sure is pouring out of my ears by now
i drown myself in the thunder of it all every day and start it all again every night

i did not ask
to be set on fire
these cups of gasoline
were forced into my hands
by strangers;
men in the streets
with cold, rough hands
their anger burning down the back of my throat
(why are they angry? why are they upset? what have i done?)
the matches swallowed in darkness as inside me,
my body implodes
"speak," they shove me unforgivingly, "speak!"
i cannot
my body is on fire, and i lie in the middle of the street
a war wages in my brain,
guns firing
smoke,
fire,
so much fire-
i cannot move.
two years later,
still stomping out the fires.
the words i have spoken have been dry, cracked and burnt
my mouth tastes like ash and smoke and my throat burns with gasoline
i am stained on the inside, i feel broken and ruined
the men have left the streets- they lost interest
two years
and i am still burning.

(every day) do you ever miss someone so much it's like an actual pain in your body ripping you apart at the seams and it's all you can do to physically wrap your arms around yourself to hold your body together
or like there's a hole in your chest. right in the middle. a giant fucking hole in your chest and it spreads sometimes and it's a giant void of everything wrong and you feel like it's going to take over you and you can't breathe and you're shaking but don't worry because ***it's all okay***

i can't handle myself

if you google "how to deal with grief", people will tell you to accept it. they will tell you to sleep, to eat, and to talk about it. they will say: "it's okay. you can be sad. these things happen." they will tell you: "things will get better."

but what they won't tell you is that grief is a monster. they won't say that one moment you'll be fine, and the next you're shaking so hard you've dropped your glass and you're on the floor. they won't tell you that you'll constantly want to tear yourself apart. that you'll blame yourself. you'll never sleep. eating is pointless. nightmares haunt you in the daytime now.

they won't tell you: that person is dead, and they're never coming back. they won't tell you: crying doesn't help. they won't tell you: there's nothing you can do but hate yourself and wish you were them.

grief is a monster. and it'll leave, then come back months later and drag you under. you'll drown all over again.

"depression"
is written on the clipboard in her hands.
followed by grief,
"anxiety",
and "emotion regulation."
people are screaming in my mind.
my blood is on fire but i don't care
this is hell
this place
i ignore the words she speaks
and focus on how i've been digging my nails into my palm so long
that little crescents have formed
and blood is welling up
she doesn't notice as i smile
and nod.

anger.
why the *fuck* does she keep saying
"everybody goes through this"
"we made you a therapy appointment why are you still sad"
yes i know
everyone has bad days
i fucking know
but not everyone's bad day ends with them wanting to die
and a therapy session won't magically fix that
and she keeps ignoring everything
and i can never breathe
and i can't stop yelling and pushing
and the people i love are leaving
and, and, and
i hate this
i hate everything
i hate and i hate and i hate
it hurts,
and i hate

sadness.
why the *hell* is it
that when it all burns out
the only thing i have energy to do is cry
the only physical reaction i can muster
is *tears*
the only thing i show is *weakness*
when only minutes-
seconds- before
i was aflame?
and even though i was setting fire to anyone close to me,
i was burning.
and then it's over
and there is nothing inside me
and everyone i love is leaving
and i can't stop collapsing in on myself
and, and, and
i hurt
i hurt, i hurt, i hurt
i hate,
and it hurts

how easily i forgot those around me
how easily i managed to erase my own identity
to lose recognition of the girl in the mirror
to trace your name on my lips
until you were the only thing my tongue could remember

how hard it was to accept the hands around me
how hard i fought to stay in the water as they tried to stop me from drowning
to keep choking on what i thought was air
to keep spitting your name out over and over
even as it made me bleed

and even now
how long it has taken
for me to stop shedding tears when you come up in a conversation
the months
until i could train my lips to speak my own name without shame
the time
it takes
to forget
is so much longer than the time it takes to remember.

he adds you on facebook.
you sit,
numb,
as your mother brushes your hair.
you can feel her questions
in the touch of her fingers
as she gently works through the tangles.
you can't make yourself say his name
it travels up your throat
with the taste of gasoline
and dies at your lips
as you cough out nothing but smoke.
you wish
furtively
that you had the same anger you did at 15,
the pride at 16.
but this
this is almost 18,
almost four years later
and the blinking notification on the screen
a reminder of
the short five minutes,
the summer before your senior year
that notification, that reminder,
it digs its way into your stomach
and sends tendrils up
to wrap around your ribs, lungs, heart
you can only sit
and stare,
gasping for breath,
begging to feel.

you went
from hand holding and singing
to avoiding eye contact
and telling your friends i was the villain
you went
from confessing your love on my 16th birthday
with a ukulele in your hands
and a song on your lips
to flinching when i spoke to you
and destroying any evidence
of us

i don't say the word
my voice stops working
every time i try to describe--
(there are no words)
half the time i cry
half the time i throw up

i still feel
absolutely disgusting
like no amount of showers
can get your scent
off my skin

knowing you left marks on me
knowing you may have left more

it wells up inside me
this monster
touching all of me
and ruining it

the final blow comes
when my mother asks
quietly
if a condom was used
and i answer

"i don't know"

i am eleven
and her lips look like fire.
she listens to the words i say
and spits them back at me
in a way that strikes my heart
but i don't understand the feeling.

i am fourteen
and i have kissed the clouds.
i hold hands with an angel
and i walk through the halls
with her by my side.

i am sixteen
and i am in love with a girl
who is a sunflower.
she brushes my hair
and comments on the freckles
on my neck.

i am eleven
and i do not like a boy.
i don't tell the girls
that my crush is the new girl down the street-
sophia-
because her hands are smooth
and she sings to me.

i am fourteen
and i can no longer attend church.
i find god
in my girlfriend
and faith in the stolen kisses,
never in school,
never in public.

i am sixteen.
i have had a boyfriend.
i loved him
the way
i love
her.

what does she have
that i don't

PART TWO- the ashes

i have lost
many people
some of whom
are still a part of me

i have constructed
many identities
none of which
are still a part of me

and i have burned
many fires
none of which
are still burning in me

your emotions confuse me
i never know
how you truly feel
(or if you even feel at all)

so i tell you every day
that i love you
so no matter what
i know you know
i am always here

and you tell me every day
that you know.

as confusing as you may be
at least
i know how to love you.

i have given up
i think
on finding a soulmate
maybe she is out there
maybe he is looking for me
but i fear
i am too complicated-
i am making this up-
i cannot choose-
i am stuck-
it's just a phase-
i fear
i am wrong
and they are right

i am so full
of so many things
because of you.
flowers, warmth
and poetry-
so much poetry
and i cannot bear
at the thought of giving it all back.
i am sorry,
for i know it is selfish,
but you cannot leave me empty.
you cannot retake these gifts
that you gave
and walk away with them.
i shake, with fear,
when i think of the hollowness
i would be.

and so
this is how the world ends.
there is the quiet hum of the wind for some far off place
and the sound of footsteps as she walks away
not even a goodbye,
not even a murmured assurance
but simply
a leaving
simply
a leaving
simply
the rain
this is not a fire
this is simply
standing. alone
it is not simple,
of course,
nothing is
yet you can't help
but feel
if she loved you
she'd simply
stay

i feel like
i work during the day
to be at my absolute best
and by the time
the night comes
i simply don't have the energy
to pretend to be anything but
exhausted

and every night
it feels like everything is ending
and every night
i cry
and as i eventually sleep
i know
i will wake up
and do the whole thing again

"me too"
every february
my friend wakes in the cold
and slowly puts on enough layers
until she feels not only warm
but safe.

until she knows she is not
the same as the 12 year old girl
in the frozen february weather
four layers on
still up for grabs
in the eyes of men

four years later

four

she tells me:

> It was 40 degrees. I was wearing 2 shirts, a jacket, jeans, a hat and a scarf. but I must have been asking for it.

she tells me:

> I live in constant fear. Fear that he will show up in my life one day. Fear I'll pass him on the street, have a mutual friend, or that I do know him and just don't recognize him.
> Fear that he's done this to someone else.

she tells me:

> Me, too.

i saw you today
biking on campus
and my heart ached

i don't even know
if you saw me
as you passed by
so quickly-

but for a moment
your face seemed still-
frozen in time
i could see every freckle.

and then
time resumed,
and as soon
as i opened my mouth
to utter a noise of surprise,

i had lost you again.

i have spent
all years of my life
accepting the quiet murmurs
in the back of my head
telling me what i know-
you are unlovable
i know
there is something about my soul
some anger
some broken sadness
where it suddenly became
too much
and i have lost the ability
for anyone to fall in love with me
to have any hope of fixing
i know they look at me
and see a bird too close to death
to ever be able to fly again

i glance at the clock-
four am
i glance at my phone
you have called me twice tonight
we talked. you said you needed to sleep.
i am awake because i know-
you're worried
whether about yourself or me this time
i don't know
but i do know
there is always the possibility
that one of us won't be there to say good morning.
and i do know
that i have to stay
and see you tomorrow morning
i have to kiss you
one more time
every night i say just one more time
if it gets us through the day.
there are scars on your arm
because we are different.
because two girls
can't love each other
the way we do.
so every night
i wait up
because i know
you're worried
that one of us won't make it through the night.

if i am just
laying there,
if i am not awake,
if you are choking me
too hard
for me to say no,
this isn't sex.

if i am simply motionless,
waiting for you
to finish
what you are doing
so i can leave,
this isn't sex.

if the only noises
you hear from me
at *all*
are of pain,
this
isn't
sex.

no. we did not sleep together.
you took my body.
we did not have sex.
you violated all rules for your own pleasure.

so no.
do not tell me i am lucky.
for what you "didn't" do.
you are lucky
i did not hurt you back.

beth wears
the flowers for a boy she lost
as a freshman
in the crook of her arm
a boy she lost
a haunting memory she carried
and tried to replace
in the arms of grown men
for years after

death is not a concept
when you are a child-
death is not something that touches your life
even in the smallest way

when he said "i love you"
she did not expect it to be some of the last words
she heard from him.

sometimes i think of her
and i want to tell her
that forgiveness is an option
and beauty still remains.

i should not
have to leave
to make you want me

i should not
have to withhold
all that i give you
for you to realize
you miss me

love should not be given
only when something is gone

i deserve love
before i leave
i deserve love
when i am here

i wear you
like a necklace

you're constantly
wrapped around my neck

you make up for it
by reaching deep within me
and planting flowers
that grow so big
i can't breathe

but god, are they beautiful

"i think,"
my mother says to me one day
"we should have a garden"

PART THREE- the garden

my poetry is not meant to caress you.
i write so it feels like
a punch in the gut.
i throw words around
like knives.
i want this to wake you up.
i want this to be absolutely
fucking
brutal.

coffee
and cigarettes
in my hands
as i move forward
----
coffee
and cigarettes
take your place
in the morning
----
coffee
and cigarettes
replace the taste of you
in my mouth
----
coffee
and cigarettes
help me say your name
without shaking
----
coffee
and cigarettes
are bitter
so i don't have to be
----
coffee
and cigarettes
are better for me
than you ever were.

she's useless without her sleep
she drinks coffee
like it's the one thing she needs more than a kiss from me
she calls me love
and darling
and doll.
her hands are rough
(she spends too much time in places she shouldn't be)
i love the feeling
of the calloused skin on her fingers
brushing on my thigh.
(she tends to wander more often than not)
she reminds me
of a honey bee
sweet yet
stinging, laughing,
knowing you've fallen in love
knowing you're only another flower
among the thousands.

it's twofold-
i want to keep you in my life
but i have to change
and recreate
the space you take up

so i focus on my friends
and a beautiful girl
and as i grow and shift,
so do you

and two phone calls
(with many tears)
later,
i understand.

i love you,
and you love me,
and the only reason
this worked
is because
i put myself first.

i lied
when i said
i cannot write poetry about you

the truth is
my hands are so full
of so many words

i could write thousands of novels
about the way
your hair looks
and your voice sounds
when you first wake up

like sunshine

i have endless descriptions
of the way you move,
the way you exist
within a room or space

i don't write you these poems.
i am scared
if i start
the words won't stop

(and regardless, i know what you'll think of them)

every inch of you as beautiful as the last
every syllable you speak, rolling over me in waves
your arms encircling me,
and i am not afraid anymore.
your laugh like the ocean, bubbling out of you with the stars in your eyes
you are as strong as the wind and as beautiful as an evergreen
i hope the sun always shines on you to grow
and there is never a storm to upset the light in your eyes
and that you always love me
the way that you do now-
fiercely, wonderfully, beautifully.

i will always be here to walk you through this life.

i had to learn to fly by falling
and i had to know how it felt
to hit the ground

i had to break
in order to mend
and i had to burn
in order to grow

sometimes
in order to learn how to swim
you have to feel like you're drowning first

i will build myself up
from the ashes you left
i will begin again
small
and green
and i will grow
tall and strong
i will water
my own roots
i will have
my own flowers

i will-
i will-
i will-
i will become
better
i can-
i will-
i have
grown
stronger
already

it took me nineteen years
to learn to love fearlessly
to be comfortable
seeing girls as flowers
and boys as rivers
and fall in love
with both
equally
it took me eighteen years
to realize hatred
and fear
should not rule my existence
it took losing friendships
it took heartbreak
it took
immense
amounts of pain
for me to learn the most important person i can love
is myself
the way
i am.
i have never loved anything less than everyone

do not flinch
when you hear them say
"i would never let a man do that"
you did not
let
anyone. do anything.
do not flinch
when they shame
for not reporting.
you did
what you had to do
to keep yourself safe.
remember
your body is sacred
a temple is sacred no matter who enters-
they will exit-
and you will still remain.
a forest can burn down
and regrow.
a garden
can have flowers plucked
by the most vile of men
and we will still
think it beautiful.

if simply the concept of me makes you run away
if simply the idea of me
is enough to make you hesitate
if simply
the thought
scares you
you are a child
and i have news for you
i am a force
a wave,
threatening to crash down on you
i am fire
a burning fire
changing everything you knew to ash
i am
your reckoning

she is
peachy love
and holding hands
flower picking with gentle petals
she is gentle words
she is the mother you never had
the color yellow
afternoon sunlight
cascading over plants on the windowsill
she has a sense
of soft nostalgia
she is pressed flowers
and oversized sweaters
and dancing around the kitchen at night

and she is fierce.
she is the stars in the night sky
and she is the sparks
as you start a lighter
she is aching and wanting
she is trying
and failing
and trying again
she is emotions
and passion and burning
she is
an adventure
wrapped up in a girl

how can you write a poem
about a patch of flowers
on the side of the road
when you're driving-
and the view to your right
is a vast, expansive sea
and yet when you pull over
it's to gently feel
the petals
and to smile-
because beauty exists-
in the least likely of spaces

how do you describe
a girl so gentle
she seems to flow
straight from the earth
a girl who stands
like an redwood tree
so strong
and so welcoming
because strength exists
in the most beautiful of places

how can you explain
a voice so melodic
you almost think you may be dreaming
you don't understand
how joy
and pain
can exist simultaneously,
so beautifully,
because vulnerability exists
even in the most strong women.

my mother was forged
in the flames of a star
in the strong voice of her mother
the sharp eyes of her father
the anger is there
in the hard set lines when she frowns
and when she yells
the world shakes

it is the way
she carries the pain
of generations before her
yet her shoulders
set back
chin up
voice steady
it is the way she moves
like she was born of this earth
the rocks itself

it is also
the way she dances
to her favorite songs
and holds my hand
as we walk together
the way her voice sits in the back of my mind
whispering encouragement
over the noise of
my own self doubt

and it is the way
when everything has fallen
and i am standing in a world
of shattered pieces
she is the one thing
that remains
whole

i have to
ease
back into poetry

it is hard
to make the words dance
like i used to

my writing feels
stiff, stilted;
disjointed

as i stretch old
muscles
and awaken
deeper areas in my brain

poetry has never been easy
but even now
as i dip my pen
back into the ink
after almost a year

it may not be easy
but it is right

you took my heart
and held it in your hands
i saw every flaw
we examined
every bump
every scrape
crack
break,
cut-

and then i took your brain. from your head
and held it in my hands
and we examined it
together
every incident
every moment you were shaken
bruised
hurt
angry
confused,

and unlike
any other boy
you gave me back my heart.
you told me you love me
and i carefully returned
your brain
to your head

you explained to me
why you could only say it then
and i understood.

and i made sure to say
"i love you too"
before hanging up the phone

i wear my pajamas to class
joggers
tshirt
oversized sweatshirt.
i run a brush through my hair
once
twice
done.
i smile at my naked face in the mirror
as i layer on chapstick.

this is what it means
to fall in love with yourself.

you are not
failing *anybody*
by waiting
to talk about it-
least of all yourself

you are not
betraying
a *single* person
if you choose not to report

and you are not
faking
any part of your pain

everything you feel-
the fear
anger
sadness
or don't feel-
the numbing
cold
grey-
is your right

you did not ask for this.

to the young girl-
you knew
you were different
as a kid

you longed for girls
the soft curves
loud voices
long fingers in your hair

you tried to fix it
therapists tried to fix it
doctors, preachers,
and most disgustingly,
neighbors
all offered to help fix it

but,
my love,
there is nothing to fix

your brain was made
like this
on purpose

you have
a special kind of love
stored up inside of you

and one day
you will meet a special kind of girl.

and she will show you
that you are not broken
and she will love you
the way you love
her.

i write
at this point
to get the words out of my head

i do not care
if my poetry is beautiful,
or even good-
i am not writing for anyone
but myself.

fuck your ego.

writing is hard-
it's like creating
your soul
from dust and dirt
only words
and whatever feeling
you put
behind them

i am slowly learning
that the girl i was
deserves my love

i am slowly trying
to extend my arms to her
and welcome her in

because the fear she feels
the loneliness
that is what got me here

but the love
and the courage
the respect

that is what will get me out

happy poetry
does not roll off my tongue
the way
words of anger do

i cannot
plant flowers
the way
i can create storms

but you give me seeds
and walk me
to a garden

and petal by petal
we create
something
beautiful

i take you to my old high school
and play you my favorite songs
reaching across the seat
as i drive
to hold your hand

as you tell me to keep talking
the music filling the space between worlds

when she smiles
it makes me feel
like there is sunlight
in my bones

and when she laughs
stars spill out
and i see
that she is the sun
the moon
and the sky
all wrapped up in a girl

falling in love
it's scary,
falling.
and i'm just starting to slip-
that moment when you lose your balance, but you haven't begun to fall yet,
and you feel it in your chest-
that's where i am

kissing him
feels like poetry
and i want to write thousands of words
with his tongue

you do not understand
the bravery in her soul.

you have not heard
the howling of the winds
you have not seen
the temple she has
in the heart of the forest
you have yet to stand
at the base of its steps
as it towers over you
gray stone set against the green of the trees
hidden deep in a maze.
you have not seen
the way she walks
flanked by wolves
her teeth just *slightly* too sharp
you sit on the throne
she is destined to usurp
cloaked in your ignorance

you do not understand
the kindness in her eyes

the same girl
with enough fire on her tongue
to burn down cities
will raise flowers from the ground

mother's day 2019
happy you day
we say jokingly in the morning
but the words ring true
we should feel this way every day
i think to myself-
appreciation for a woman so strong
she shaped our lives by hand
carefully
every detail
a woman who still shapes
still holds us in her palms
past the time she should feel any requirement to

happy you day
to the woman who built me
who helped create the next generation of women
strong, beautiful.
i love you, mom.

i never saw you as someone who would see me. i never thought of myself as the type of girl that you would look for. yet somehow you met me and kept searching into the inner depths of my soul. and you kept digging because you liked what you found in me. you made yourself at home in the nooks and crannies of my heart before i even knew what was happening. by the time i could take a full breath around you, you already owned my heart.

i wish i could say i took my time. but the truth is i jumped into you without checking to see if the water was deep enough. i let myself sink into the darkest parts. holding my breath for weeks at a time. and finally when you pulled me out i realized you were already moving into the deepest part of my heart. grabbing my hand. pulling me out of the water. only to jump back in with me again.

the best thing you have ever done for me
is taught me how to love
and how i should be loved
you showed me the way i deserve to be treated.
you raised me
in a way that kept me safe-
you raised me.
and even when i was angry
when i said i hated you
you worked to give me the life
and the father you never had.
i will never forget
the photo we have
i am in your arms, laughing
because you keep ticking me
seven years old
and you can tell
how happy i am.

i like the way you make me feel like music. swaying to deep guitars and gentle drum beats. counting the days like the rhythm of our songs. the music we make is beautiful, more beautiful than anything i could sing to you. the colors burst across my mind when i am with you.

when you look into the mirror
i hope you see the beautiful girl you are
i hope you see under all of that anger and anxiety
that you are an angel.

our first conversation
was like hearing a song for the first time
knowing all of the words
dancing to a melody you had awoken in me

you feel like walking into a place i had forgotten

they say the first love hurts the most.

may ninth. 2018.
i turned 18 years old.

you emailed me. you asked if i still wanted to get coffee. we hadn't spoken in months.
i said no.
your last words to me then were:
"maybe in another life".

may ninth. 2019.
i turned 19 years old.

you have another girlfriend. an apartment. you finished two years of college.
and i'm happy for you.

i won't lie. i checked up on you.
i spent too much of the year being angry. i spent too long letting you define me.

i don't want to be angry anymore. i want to move on.
i'm happy you're happy. and i hope you've grown. i hope you love her. and i hope she loves you.

i've grown. i love myself. i'm publishing the book that holds *so much* of you because i want to let go. there are pages of you in here. for a while, i felt like i was walking around with your name written on my tongue.

but one year later
and i am writing my own words.
here they are.

this is my goodbye.
and my hello.

the start of my own journey.

thank you for reading this book. thank you for walking on this journey with me. i love you, more than words can say, and i hope you keep fighting.

because we are never alone:

i would not have been able to write this completely by myself. i would not have been able to grow without the help of so many beautiful people around me. i would not be in the place i am today, or the person i am today, without my family and friends supporting me every step of the way.

there are too many people to name in just a few pages, so i would like to say thank you to all of you. to the people who read my poems, to the people who held my hand, to the people who let me cry and the people who danced with me when the sun was shining and the people who listened to me when i struggled to find light. and to you, for reading this.

to my family:

to my parents- laura and paul pritchard, the most inspiring people i know. i hope someday i can find a love that is even half as strong as the one you share. you two inspire me every day to get out of bed. i could not have asked for better people to raise me. above all, you have made me into the woman i am today. i carry your voices and your strength in me every day and with everything i do. you are my best friends, you are my whole heart.

my sister. ellie. you saved my life. you are the reason i strive every day to be the best version of myself i can be. every time i work to improve myself, every time i make the decision to keep fighting, it is because i am thinking of you. not only to be a strong role model for you, but because i know you believe in me. i know you always have my back. you are the strongest person i know, ellie. i hope you always have this bright and beautiful and big a role in my life.

baba and grandfather. you have always supported my writing. you have overcome countless hardships. grandfather, you inspired me to write this book. baba, you have always had my back. i love both of you endlessly.

to my friends:

maggie mundt, my mom away from home. the love and light of my life. i have never met a human so soft and gentle. maggie, you are a poem in and of yourself. you are the way the wind blows softly on a spring day. your beauty shines through every inch of your existence. you make me believe in angels because you are one.

katie, my tea provider and stand up comedy connoisseur. my crazy smart beautiful talented lovely friend. you are the floating soprano notes of the world's most beautiful song. you are the embodiment of courage. hearing your voice is like listening to the sounds of a smile. you can do anything. you have already changed the world.

thea... words do not explain the love i have for you. you are my family. by soul and spirit. you were a gift given to me by the universe. sometimes i think about your existence, your presence in my life, and i am overwhelmed by you and your love. you have been here for the darkest times and the best times and i want nothing but for you to continue to be with me for the rest of my life.

machaela. you made me believe in soulmates. you kissed me when i was 14 and my life changed. you are the color yellow. i am in love with your smile. i am struggling to come up with words to explain how much you mean to me. almost six years of knowing you is enough to make me know i will love you for every lifetime i have.

claire: you came into my life, made a space for yourself, and i hope you never leave it. you are my rock, the place i can go to at the end of a hard day. you are a constant, never-changing stream of love. you know my heart and you look out for me. i am eternally grateful for the fact that i got to meet you. i hope i never lose you.

j.r.- words quite simply cannot adequately sum up the past six years. you were always on my side, no matter what. you've seen this book since it started. if it weren't for you, these poems would still be in my journals under my bed, living as a "what if". i have loved you in every sense of the word. you have had so many roles in my life. know that from all the way back when i was a 13 year old girl writing you stumbling, messy poems, to now, you have always been someone i *know* i can rely on.

lilly... we are two sides of the same coin. i have had the distinct pleasure of growing up and watching you grow up next to me into such a strong, passionate, badass young woman. you inspire me every day to do more. you are a sunset on a summer night. you will always be a part of my life. i refuse to ever lose you. i love you so much that thinking about it almost physically overwhelms me. please know that you are perfect.

jess allen. my mentor, my wife, my best friend, my mother figure, my everything. it feels absolutely ridiculous to say i have only known you for a year, when i feel as though i've known your soul my whole life. every moment i am with you is blessed. you are my platonic other half.

> and by extension, of course, danny. you allowed me to storm into your life and even went so far as to welcome me in. you have been an invaluable source of advice, love, and support. i love you.

Made in the USA
Columbia, SC
22 January 2021

31457755R00048